Nita Mehta's

INDIAN VEGETARIAN

FAVOURITES

SNAB
Excellence in Books

Nita Mehta's **INDIAN VEGETARIAN**

FAVOURITES

Nita Mehta

B.Sc. (Home Science)
M.Sc. (Food and Nutrition), Gold Medalist

SNAB
Excellence in Books

Nita Mehta's **INDIAN VEGETARIAN FAVOURITES**

First Hardbound Edition 2009

ISBN 978-81-7869-273-9

Food Styling & Photography:

Layout and Laser Typesetting:

	National Information Technology Academy 3A/3, Asaf Ali Road New Delhi-110 002
N.I.T.A. ☎ 23252948	

Published by:

SNAB
Excellence in Books
Publishers Pvt. Ltd.
3A/3 Asaf Ali Road,
New Delhi - 110002
Tel: 23252948, 23250091
Telefax:91-11-23250091

Editorial and Marketing office:
E-159, Greater Kailash-II, N.Delhi-48
Fax: 91-11-29225218, 29229558
Tel: 91-11-29214011, 29218574
E-Mail: nitamehta@email.com
nitamehta@nitamehta.com
_Website:_http://www.nitamehta.com
Website: http://www.snabindia.com

Contributing Writers :
Anurag Mehta
Tanya Mehta

Editorial & Proofreading :
Rakesh
Ramesh

Printed at:
MANIPAL PRESS LTD

Distributed by:
THE VARIETY BOOK DEPOT
A.V.G. Bhavan, M 3 Con Circus
New Delhi - 110 001
Tel: 23417175, 23412567; Fax: 23415335
E-mail: varietybookdepot@rediffmail.com

Price: Rs. 250/-

Introduction

The true art of Indian cooking lies in the subtle use and variation of spices which makes each dish exotic and an exciting new experience. The best Indian dishes are a clever blend of exotic spices, delicate herbs and vegetables.

The main course dishes include *tandoori* foods and curries prepared from vegetables. The real *tandoor* is a very large earthenware pot which has a bed of burning charcoal inside. This imparts a smoky flavour to the food. The food to be cooked is speared on large skewers which are placed vertically in the clay pot. Today almost all Indian homes have replaced it with electric ovens or electric *tandoors*.

Indian curries are delicious and can be prepared with just a few simple ingredients. The secret of producing these aromatic delicacies is adding the right ingredient at the right time, thus following the correct sequence of cooking.

Pulses and lentils (*Dals*) form an important part of a vegetarian Indian meal. Aromatic cumin seeds dropped in hot oil and cooked on low heat till golden, added to pulses, change them completely. On the other hand, if the cumin seeds get burnt, a mess is produced. The book explains very clearly, how to flavour your pulses the right way!

The vegetables are eaten with rice or Indian breads (*roti*). Exotic *biryaanis* and *pulaos* prepared from Indian *basmati* rice, flavoured with magical spices like fennel seeds, cinnamon sticks and cardamom pods, are all explained simply.

I have tried to make the recipes as simple as possible, giving step-by-step instructions, allowing you to enjoy the exotic flavours and aroma of Indian food, any time of the week.

Nita Mehta

Contents

Legumes & Pulses   58

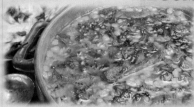

Raitas, Salads, Chutneys & Pickles   67

Rice & Breads   75

Desserts   87

Drinks

Tomato Rasam

An authentic, thin tomato soup of Southern India, delicious as an appetizer.

Serves 6-8

1 kg tomatoes - cut into 4 pieces, 3 cups water

1 tbsp oil, 2-3 whole, dry, red chillies or ½ tsp paprika

1 tsp cumin seeds *(jeera),* 1 tsp mustard seeds *(rai),* ¼ tsp asafoetida *(hing)*

a few curry leaves, ¼ tsp ground turmeric *(haldi)*

1½ tsp salt, or to taste, 1½ tsp peppercorns *(saboot kali mirch)*

1 small pod garlic, whole

1. Boil whole tomatoes with 3 cups water. Keep on low heat for about 10 minutes, till tomatoes turn soft. Remove from heat and cool. Blend to a puree.

2. Heat 1 tbsp oil. Reduce heat and fry the red chillies till they turn a shade darker. Add together — cumin seeds, mustard seeds and asafoetida. When cumin turns golden, add curry leaves.

3. Add the pureed tomatoes. Add salt and turmeric powder. Separate the flakes of garlic from the pod and crush them roughly without peeling the flakes. Separately, crush or pound the peppercorns too. Add the crushed garlic and peppercorns to the tomatoes. Boil. Simmer for 10 minutes. Remove from heat.

4. Strain. Discard the ingredients in the strainer. Serve soup garnished with coriander leaves.

Mint Lassi

This yogurt smoothie is a very popular drink in the Northern part of India, specially Punjab. There are sweet and salty versions of this Indian drink. The savoury one given here is seasoned with roasted cumin and mint whereas the delicious sweet cooler is generally flavoured with rose water and cardamoms.

Serves 4

4 tbsp finely chopped mint leaves *(pudina)*

1½ cups plain yogurt, ½ tsp rock salt *(kala namak)*

½ tsp roasted ground cumin seeds *(jeera)*, ½ tsp salt, or to taste

3 cups water, 6-8 ice cubes

1. Wash and finely chop mint leaves. Put yogurt, mint, cumin seeds, rock salt and salt in a blender. Blend for a few seconds.

2. Add chilled water and ice cubes. Blend till frothy. Serve sprinkled with a pinch of ground, roasted cumin seeds and garnished with finely chopped mint.

Thandai

A festive drink prepared from nuts and flavourful spices blended in milk.

Serves 10-12

6 cups of milk, ½ cup almonds, 2 tbsp cashews (*kaju*) - broken into bits

1/3 cup seeds of watermelon (*magaz*), 8 tbsp poppy seeds (*khus khus*)

15-20 peppercorns (*saboot kali mirch*), 10-12 green cardamoms (*chhoti illaichi*)

1 tbsp dried rose petals, 2 tsp fennel seeds (*saunf*)

10-12 tbsp sugar, a few strands of saffron (*kesar*) - soaked in 1 tsp water for garnishing

1. Soak almonds separately in water for 3-4 hours. Peel almonds. Soak together — watermelon seeds, poppy seeds, cashews, peppercorns, cardamoms, rose petals and fennel seeds for 3-4 hours. Strain.

2. Add the peeled almonds to the strained ingredients. Put all the soaked ingredients in a mixer grinder and grind to a paste by adding a little water or milk. The grinding of the ingredients should be done very well. Grind well to a smooth paste.

3. Add the ground ingredients to the cold milk. Add sugar and mix well. Strain the milk through a cheese cloth and discard the residue.

4. Chill the drink by adding ice. Serve garnished with soaked saffron strands and fresh rose petals.

This is predominantly a summer drink which aids digestion. A savoury tamarind and mint (pudina) cooler which is flavoured with roasted cumin seeds (jeera) and black salt. This tangy cooler can be made as peppery as you like.

Serves 4

4 cups water

4 tbsp seedless tamarind (*imli*), 4 tsp fresh lime juice

3 tbsp sugar, 1" ginger - crushed roughly

¼ cup fresh mint leaves (*pudina*) - minced

1½ tsp ground, roasted cumin (*bhuna jeera*), ½ tsp black salt *(kala namak)*

salt to taste, ½ tsp red chilli powder, or to taste, optional

1. Soak seedless tamarind in 1 cup hot water for 1 hour. Mash well. Add the remaining 3 cups water. Mash once again and strain to get tamarind water. If you are using tamarind pulp, add 4 cups of water to the pulp. If the pulp is salted, no salt is required in the *jeera pani*.

2. To the tamarind water, add all other ingredients — lime juice, crushed ginger, mint, black salt, ground roasted cumin, red chilli powder, sugar & salt to taste.

3. Mix well. Keep for 2 hours in the fridge to chill and for the flavours to penetrate. At serving time, strain through a fine sieve. Adjust seasonings. Serve garnished with a lemon slice and mint.

Snacks

Cocktail Gobhi Samosas

These triangular pockets of pastry filled with a spicy vegetable or curried minced meat are a popular Indian snack. They can be made substantial enough to constitute a light meal or dainty enough to serve as a cocktail savoury.

Serves 8-10

DOUGH

¾ cup plain flour (*maida*), ¼ cup fine semolina (*suji*)

¼ tsp salt, a pinch of baking powder, 30 gm (2 tbsp) ghee or butter or margarine

VEGETABLE FILLING

3 tbsp oil, 1 tbsp each raisins (*kishmish*) & cashews (*kaju*) - chopped

1 medium cauliflower - grated (2 cups), 1 boiled potato - mashed coarsely (½ cup)

½" piece fresh ginger - grated, ½ tsp red chilli powder, salt to taste

1 tsp roasted, ground cumin seeds (*jeera*), ¼ tsp dry mango powder (*amchoor*)

2 green chillies - deseeded and finely chopped, ¼ tsp sugar

1. Sift flour, semolina, salt and baking powder into a bowl. Rub in ghee or butter. Add a few tablespoons of cold water to form a firm dough. Knead for 5-7 minutes until the dough becomes smooth and elastic. Cover the dough and keep aside for 30 minutes or longer while making the filling.

2. To prepare the filling, heat 3 tbsp oil in a pan. Remove from heat. Add ginger, salt, red chilli powder, ground cumin seeds and dry mango powder.

3. Return to heat. Add cashews. Cook for a few seconds. Add potatoes. Stir for a few seconds. Add cauliflower. Mix well. Add sugar and green chillies.

4. Cover and cook on low heat till the cauliflower is cooked. Make the filling spicy if you like. Keep aside.

5. Make lemon sized balls of the dough. Roll out into thin rounds. Cut each circle in half. Brush some water on the straight edges. Pick up the half circle and form a cone shape, overlapping straight edges 6 mm/¼" and pressing firmly to seal the seam. Fill cone two-thirds with the filling, about 1 tbsp of the filling in each cone. Press together to make a secure joint.

6. Deep fry in medium hot oil till golden. Drain on absorbent paper towels and serve warm with mint or tamarind chutney.

Tip: Never fry the samosas on high heat and fry 8-10 pieces together in a single batch. If the oil is too hot, the outer covering gets browned very fast, without getting cooked properly.

Masala Dosa

Nothing is too difficult if you know all the secrets – learn to make perfect dosas with this detailed recipe. Two kinds of rice and urad dal are soaked, ground, then allowed to ferment overnight to make a light batter for the dosas.

Makes 20-25

BATTER

2 cups parboiled (*sela* or *ushna chaawal*) rice of ordinary quality

1 cup ordinary quality rice (*permal chaawal*)

1 cup split black gram dal (*dhuli urad dal*), 2 tsp fenugreek seeds (*methi dana*)

2 tsp salt, to taste, oil for making dosas

POTATO MASALA

4 medium (½ kg) potatoes - boiled, ¼ cup peas - boiled (optional)

2 tbsp oil, ¾ tsp mustard seeds (*sarson*), 1 tsp bengal gram dal (*channe ki dal*)

1 dry, red chilli - broken into pieces, few curry leaves

2 green chillies - chopped, ¼" piece of ginger - chopped

2 small onions - chopped, 1 tbsp cashewnuts (*kaju*) - broken into bits

¼ tsp turmeric (*haldi*) powder, ¼ tsp red chilli powder, salt to taste

1. To prepare the batter, soak both the rice, dal and fenugreek seeds together in a pan for at least 6 hours.

2. Grind together finely to a paste, using some of the water in which it was soaked.

3. Add more water to the paste, if required, to get a paste of medium pouring consistency.

4. Add salt. Mix well.

5. Keep aside for 12 hours or overnight in a warm place, to get fermented. After fermentation, the batter rises a little and smells sour.

6. After the batter is ready, prepare the masala. Boil the potatoes. Peel and mash them roughly.

7. Heat 2 tbsp oil in a *kadhai*. Reduce flame and add ¾ tsp sarson, 1 tsp bengal gram dal and 1 dry red chilli.

8. When dal changes colour, add curry leaves, ginger, green chilli Stir fry for 2 minutes on low flame.

9. Add onion. Cook till transparent. Add cashewnuts, salt, turmeric and red chilli powder. Fry for 1 minute.

10. Add 1 cup water. Boil and keep covered on low flame for 5-7 minutes or till the dal turns soft.

11. Add the mashed potatoes and peas. Cook for 5 minutes. Mix well. Remove from fire. Keep masala aside.

12. To prepare the dosa, mix the batter nicely with a *karchhi*.

13. Heat a non stick *tawa* on medium flame. Pour a tsp oil on the *tawa* and rub the oil with piece of old cloth.

14. Remove the pan from fire and pour 1 heaped karchhi of batter. Spread quickly, but lightly.

15. Return to fire. Cook till the dosa gets a little cooked.

16. Pour 2 tsp of oil upon the dosa and on the sides.

17. After golden brown spots appear, gently loosen the sides and the bottom.

18. Put 2 tbsp masala in the centre and spread a little. Fold over from both sides. Remove from *tawa*.

19. Place a blob of white butter on the dosa and serve hot with coconut chutney and sambar. Serve pudina and tomato chutney also if you have the time to prepare them.

Kathi Rolls

Wraps of soya granules flavoured with fresh coriander and mint.

Makes 8-10

8-10 roomali rotis or thin home made large rotis (wrap rotis in aluminium foil and put in a casserole)

1 cup thin sticks of cucumber (*kheera*) and 1 cup carrot sticks - to pickle

½ cup water, ½ cup white vinegar, ½ tsp salt, ½ tsp sugar

FILLING

1 cup nutri nuggets granules - soaked in 2 cups hot water for ½ hour

2 tbsp oil, ½ tsp cumin seeds (*jeera*), ¼ tsp nigella seeds (*kalonji*)

2 green chillies - chopped

4 onions - each cut into half and then widthwise to get half rings

½ tsp turmeric (*haldi*) powder, ½ tsp dry mango powder (*amchoor*)

3 tbsp tomato ketchup

¾ cup chopped coriander, 4 tbsp mint (*pudina*) - chopped roughly or torn with hands

2 capsicums - cut into 1" long, thin strips

1 tomato - deseeded & cut into 1" long, thin strips

1½ tsp salt, ¼ tsp pepper powder, ¾ tsp garam masala, ½ tsp red chilli powder

1. For the pickled veggies, mix water, vinegar, salt and sugar in a deep pan. Bring to a boil. Take the pan off the fire and add carrots and cucumber. Keep in the vinegar to cool.

2. For making the filling of kathi rolls, heat 1 tbsp oil in a pan, add cumin seeds and nigella seeds. Wait till cumin seeds turns golden. Add green chillies, fry for ½ minute on medium flame (do not brown them), add onions and stir till transparent on low heat for 5-7 minutes. Add nuggets, ½ tsp turmeric powder and dry mango powder. Stir on low heat for 5 minutes. Add ketchup, coriander and mint. Mix for 1-2 minutes.

3. Add capsicum and cook for a minute. Add salt, pepper powder, garam masala and red chilli powder. Cook for 2-3 minutes. Lastly add the tomato fingers and mix lightly. Remove from fire.

4. To assemble the kathi roll, take one roomali roti. Place some filling in the centre. Put some pickled veggies on it. Fold the sides to get a roll. Heat 1 tbsp oil in a pan and warm the roll by putting the joint side down in oil first. Turn carefully with a flat spoon when light golden from the bottom. Pan fry for a minute. Serve with hari chutney and some pickled veggies.

Rava Idli

Urad dal is soaked and ground; rava (suji) is soaked in curd and then ground; they are mixed together and fermented overnight to make the batter for these outstanding idlis.

Makes 15

1 cup split black gram (*urad dhuli dal*), 2 cups semolina (*rava suji*)
½ cup sour curd, 1½ -2 tsp salt or to taste

1. Soak the dal for at least 2 hours or more.

2. Soak rava in curd. Add enough water to soak the rava. Mash it nicely with the fingers. Soak for at least ½ hour.

3. Grind dal to a very fine paste with a little water. Even after you feel that the dal is ready, grind some more adding a little water in-between till the dal turns absolutely smooth and fluffy and a few bubbles can be seen.

4. Add rava to the dal batter. Add salt. The batter should be of a thick pouring consistency.

5. Keep the batter for 8-10 hours in a warm place to get fermented. Cover with a shawl in winters. After fermentation, the batter rises and smells a little sour. Keep the batter away for a longer time if it does not ferment properly.

6. To make idlis, mix the batter very gently. Wash idli mould. Do not wipe. Grease the mould with oil. Fill with batter.

7. Put 1" water in a big cooker or a big pan with a well fitting lid and place on the gas. Keep it on fire.

8. Place the idli mould inside the cooker and put the lid after removing the whistle. Keep the gas on full flame.

9. After water boils and the steam starts coming out, reduce flame. Keep for 15 minutes on medium flame. Insert a clean knife to see if the idli is done. If it sticks to the knife, steam for another 3-4 minutes.

10. Switch off the gas and remove the idlis from the mould after cooling for 5 minutes, with a clean knife.

11. Serve hot with chutney and sambar.

Note: Dhuli urad dal should be ground very well adding little water in-between while grinding, otherwise the Idli will not be soft.

Paneer Tikka

Soft pieces of paneer smeared with a flavoured yogurt paste and put in a tandoor or grilled in an oven to get a crisp and succulent snack.

Serves 4

250 gm *paneer* - cut into ¼"/6 mm thick 1"/2.5 cm square pieces

1 capsicum - cut into rings, 2 onions - cut into rings 1"/2.5 cm ginger

3-4 flakes garlic, 1-2 dried, whole red chilli

2 tbsp drained thick yogurt - (hang ¼ cup yogurt for 15 minutes), 2 tbsp thick cream

a few drops of orange colour or a pinch of turmeric, 1 tsp lemon juice, 3 tbsp oil

½ tsp rock salt *(kala namak)*, 1 tsp *tandoori masala*, ½ tsp salt, or to taste

¼ tsp ground cumin seeds *(jeera powder)*, 1 tomato - cut into thick slices to garnish

1. Grind ginger, garlic and chillies to a paste. To the paste, add hung yogurt, cream, ground cumin, lemon juice, 2 tbsp oil, salt, rock salt, tandoori masala and colour or ground turmeric. Marinate *paneer*, capsicum and onion pieces in it for at least 2 hours.

2. At the time of serving, grill *paneer* pieces and vegetables by placing them on a grill rack brushed with some oil. After 5-7 minutes, when the *paneer* turns golden at the edges, turn sides.

3. Grill the *paneer* for 3-4 minutes till it starts getting crisp from this side also. Remove the vegetables and the *paneer* from the oven. Arrange hot *paneer* in a serving platter and surround with onions, capsicums and tomato rings.

Gulnar Seekh Kabab

Succulent vegetarian kebabs prepared from lentils. The colourful peppers on the outer surface give it an exotic look.

Makes 15

1 cup split red lentils (*dhuli masoor ki dal*)

1"/2.5 cm piece ginger, 8-10 flakes garlic

1 tsp cumin seeds (*jeera*), 1 tsp garam masala, 1 tsp red chilli powder

3 slices bread - dipped in water & squeezed well

1 tsp salt, or to taste, 3 tbsp oil

2 tbsp each of finely chopped green pepper, onion and red pepper

TO SERVE

2 onions - cut into rings, juice of 1 lemon, a few mint leaves (*pudina*) - finely chopped

1. Soak lentils for 2 hours. Strain. Grind lentils, ginger, garlic and cumin seeds to a thick paste using the minimum amount of water. Keep the ground lentil paste aside.

2. Heat 3 tbsp oil in a heavy bottomed wok or a non stick pan. Add the lentil paste. Stir-fry for 4-5 minutes on low heat till lentils turn dry and stop sticking to the bottom of the pan. Remove from heat.

3. Remove sides of bread and dip in water for a second. Squeeze well and crumble finely. Mix bread, salt, garam masala and red chilli powder with the lentils. Mix well. Keep aside.

4. Heat oil in a pan for frying the kebabs. Grease a wooden or a metal skewer. Spread a ball of lentil paste along the length of the skewer, such that it is inserted in the roll. Make a finger thick, 2"/5 cm long kabab of the lentil paste on the skewer.

5. Stick finely chopped onion and peppers on the kabab on the skewer, by pressing them on to the kabab.

6. Gently pull out the skewer and fry the seekh in medium hot oil till golden brown. Serve hot on a bed of onion rings sprinkled with lemon juice and chopped mint leaves.

Vegetable & Fruit Chaat

A delicious vegetable & fruit mix tossed with chaat masala and lemon. In the absence of chaat masala, freshly ground black pepper and black salt can be substituted, although you will miss out on the real taste.

Serves 6

2 boiled potatoes - cut into 1" pieces, 1 small cucumber - cut into 1" pieces

1 tomato - cut into cubes & pulp removed

1 cup fresh pomegranate kernels (*anaar ke daane*)

1 banana - cut into slices, 1 apple - cut into 1" pieces

1 tbsp *chaat masala,* or to taste, 2 tbsp lemon juice

oil for frying

1. Heat oil in a pan. Add the boiled potatoes. Fry potatoes to a rich brown colour. Remove from oil on an absorbent paper napkin.

2. Mix all the other fruits and vegetables in a large mixing bowl. Add the fried potatoes. Sprinkle *chaat masala* and lemon juice. Toss gently. Serve.

VEGETARIAN Curries

Malai Mushroom Matar

*This milk-based, fragrant gravy will not overpower the delicacy of mushrooms and peas
– a gourmet-class dish made in minutes.*

Serves 4-5

200 gm mushrooms - preferably small in size

1 cup shelled, boiled or frozen peas, 4 tbsp dry fenugreek leaves (*kasoori methi*)

1 tsp ginger-garlic paste, a pinch of pepper, 1 tbsp butter, 3 tbsp oil

2 onions - ground to a paste

¼ cup malai - mix with ¼ cup milk and blend in a mixer for a few seconds till smooth or
½ cup thin fresh cream, 1 tsp salt to taste

½ tsp red chilli powder, ½ tsp garam masala, a pinch of amchoor, ½ cup milk (approx.)

GRIND TOGETHER

½ stick cinnamon (*dalchini*), seeds of 2-3 green cardamom (*chhoti illaichi*)

3-4 cloves (*laung*), 4-5 peppercorns (*saboot kali mirch*)

2 tbsp roasted gram (*bhuna channa*) or cashewnuts

1. Trim the stem of each mushroom. Leave them whole if small or cut them into 2 pieces, if big. Heat 1 tbsp butter in a kadhai and add the mushrooms. Stir fry on high flame till dry and golden. Add 1 tsp ginger-garlic paste, ½ tsp salt and a pinch of black pepper. Stir for 1 more minute and remove from fire. Keep cooked mushrooms aside.

2. Grind together cinnamon, seeds of green cardamom, cloves, peppercorns and channa/cashew to a powder in a small mixer grinder.

3. Heat 3 tbsp oil. Add onion paste and cook on low heat till oil separates. Do not let the onions turn brown.

4. Add the freshly ground masala powder. Cook for a few seconds.

5. Add dry fenugreek leaves and malai, cook on low heat for 2-3 minutes till malai dries.

6. Add salt, red chilli powder, garam masala and amchoor. Stir for 1 minute.

7. Add the boiled peas and mushrooms.

8. Add ½ cup milk to get a thick gravy. Add ½ cup water if the gravy appears too thick. Boil for 2-3 minutes. Serve.

Paalak Makai

Serves 4

500 gm spinach (*paalak*), 1 cup cooked corn kernels

1" piece ginger - grated, 3 tbsp oil or ghee, 2 black cardamoms (*moti illaichi*)

1" stick cinnamon (*dalchini*), 5-6 flakes garlic - crushed to a rough paste

2 onions - finely sliced, 3 tomatoes - chopped

¾ tsp turmeric powder (*haldi*), 1 tsp ground coriander (*dhania*)

½ tsp red chilli powder, ½ tsp garam masala, 1 tsp salt, or to taste

1. Boil whole fresh corn or frozen corn kernels with ¼ tsp turmeric, 2 tsp sugar and 1 tsp salt to get soft, yellow, sweetish corn. If using tinned corn, simply drain the water and use.

2. Heat oil. Reduce heat. Add black cardamoms & cinnamon. Wait for a minute.

3. Add garlic and cook till it starts to change colour. Add onions and stir fry till golden. Reduce heat.

4. Add turmeric powder, coriander powder, chilli powder, garam masala and salt. Mix well on low heat for a minute.

5. Add ginger. Stir for a few seconds. Add corn. Stir fry for 2-3 minutes.

6. Add spinach. Continue cooking, without covering, for about 10 minutes, till the spinach gets wilted and is well blended with the corn.

7. Add tomatoes and stir fry for 3-4 minutes. Garnish with ginger match sticks and serve hot with chappatis.

Paneer Makhani

Paneer is added to a fragrant tomato curry cooked in butter. You may substitute paneer with potatoes and peas if you like and turn it into makhani aloo matar.

Serves 6

250 gm *paneer* - cut into 1"/2.5 cm pieces

GRAVY

3 tbsp butter or oil

2 onions - chopped (1 cup), 1 tsp chopped ginger

½ tsp red chilli powder, 6-7 tomatoes (500 gm) - chopped

¼ cup yogurt - whisked till smooth

3 tbsp cashews (*kaju*) - soaked in a little water for 15 minutes & ground to a paste

¼ tsp ground nutmeg, optional, 1½ tsp salt, or to taste, ¾ tsp garam masala

½-1 tsp sugar, or to taste, ½ cup thin fresh cream or milk

1 tbsp tomato ketchup

1. Heat 2 tbsp butter or oil in a pan. Add onions and ginger. Cook on low heat until onions turn transparent. Add red chilli powder. Stir. Add chopped tomatoes. Cover and cook for 7-8 minutes till the tomatoes turn pulpy.

2. Add yogurt. Cook till the mixture turns dry and reddish again.

3. Remove from heat. Cool. Grind to a very smooth puree with ½ cup water. Heat 1 tbsp of butter or oil in a wok or a deep pan. Add the prepared tomato-yogurt puree. Stir fry for 3-4 minutes on low heat.

4. Add salt, garam masala, sugar and tomato ketchup. Mix. Add cashew paste. Cook on low heat for 1-2 minutes.

5. Add enough milk or very thin fresh cream, to get a thick pouring consistency of the gravy. Add *paneer* pieces. Give one boil on low heat. Remove from heat. Transfer to a serving dish.

6. Garnish with a swirl of cream, a few coriander leaves and ginger match-sticks. Serve with nans, paranthas or any other bread.

Shahi Kaaju Aloo

Potatoes are simmered in a delicious, white gravy. Curd and cashews form the base of this royal (shahi) curry. Black cumin lends it's royal flavour to the humble potatoes.

Serves 8-10

300 gm (4) potatoes

4 tbsp cashews (*kaju*) - soaked in ¼ cup water

1 tbsp chopped ginger, 1 tsp chopped garlic

½ tsp black cumin (*shah jeera*), 1 bay leaf (*tej patta*)

2 onions - chopped (1 cup)

a pinch of turmeric (*haldi*), ¼ tsp garam masala

2 tbsp chopped coriander

¼ cup yogurt - whisked to make it smooth, ¼ cup milk

oil for frying and 4 tbsp oil

1. Wash potatoes and peel. Cut potatoes into 1"/2.5 cm pieces.

2. Fry the potatoes to a deep golden brown and keep aside. Grind cashews, ginger and garlic to a paste in a small coffee or spice grinder. Keep cashew paste aside.

3. Heat 4 tbsp oil in a heavy bottomed pan. Add black cumin and bay leaf. Wait for 30 seconds till cumin stops spluttering. Add onions and cook on low heat till onions turn soft but do not let them turn brown. Add turmeric and garam masala. Stir to mix well.

4. Add cashew paste. Cook for 1 minute. Add yogurt and stir fry till water evaporates. Cook till dry.

5. Add milk and about ½ cup water to get a gravy. Boil and simmer for 2-3 minutes.

6. Add the fried potatoes and chopped coriander to the gravy and simmer on low heat.

7. Cook on low heat till the gravy gets thick and coats the potatoes. Serve hot with rotis or paranthas.

Gujarati Kadi

Serves 2-3

1 cup yogurt (*dahi*)

1 tbsp gram flour (*besan*), 1 cup water

¾ tsp salt, ½ tsp ginger-green chilli paste

1 tsp sugar, a pinch of turmeric (*haldi*)

TEMPERING

1 tbsp oil

seeds of 1 green cardamom (*chhoti illaichi*)

½ tsp cumin seeds (*jeera*)

½" cinnamon (*dalchini*)

2 cloves (*laung*) - crushed

8-10 curry leaves

¼ tsp red chilli powder

1. Mix 1 tbsp gram flour with 1 cup curd. Add 1 cup water. Mix well to remove any lumps.

2. Heat oil in a *kadhai*, add ginger-green chilli paste. Cook for a minute.

3. Add gramflour mixture, salt, sugar and turmeric. Bring to a boil and then reduce heat and cook 10-15, stirring in between.

4. For tempering, heat oil in a pan, add cumin seeds, cinnamon, cloves and curry leaves. Cook till cumin turns golden.

5. Immediately add ¼ tsp red chilli powder to the hot oil, mix well and pour over the kadi. Serve hot.

Kofta Rangeen

Potato dumplings (koftas) with colourful vegetable filling. The colours are exposed by dividing each kofta into two. Served on a bed of red, cardamom flavoured curry.

Serves 4

KOFTA COVERING

4 slices bread - dipped in water & squeezed, 4 potatoes - boiled & grated (2 cups)
¾ tsp salt, or to taste, ½ tsp black pepper, pinch of baking powder, 2 tsp tomato ketchup

KOFTA FILLING

1 carrot - grated thickly (½ cup), 1 capsicum - shredded (½ cup)
3-4 tbsp shredded green cabbage, ¼ cup grated cheddar cheese, salt, pepper to taste

GRAVY

4 tbsp oil, 2 black cardamoms (*moti illaichi*), 2 onions - chopped (1 cup)
3 tomatoes - chopped (1½ cups), 2 tsp finely grated ginger
1½ tsp ground coriander (*dhania powder*), ½ tsp each red chilli powder & garam masala
¾ cup milk, 1 tbsp tomato ketchup, salt to taste

1. For the kofta covering, in a bowl mix potatoes with all the ingredients till well blended. Divide into 4 big balls. Keep aside. For the filling, mix all the vegetables with cheese together. Sprinkle some salt and pepper to taste.

2. Flatten each potato ball to a size of about 3"/8 cm diameter. Place 1 tbsp of filling in the centre. Lift the sides to cover the filling. Give the kofta an oval shape like an egg. Deep fry koftas, one at a time, carefully till golden brown.

3. To prepare the gravy, grind onions, tomatoes and ginger together. Heat oil. Add cardamoms and wait for 30-40 seconds. Add onion-tomato paste and cook on medium heat till well dried. Add ground coriander and red chilli powder. Stir fry till oil comes to the surface.

4. Reduce heat. Add milk gradually, 2-3 tbsp at a time, stirring continuously till all the milk is used. Cook on low heat till the mixture turns red again and the oil separates. Add enough water to get a thin curry. Boil. Add salt, garam masala, tomato ketchup and cook on low heat for 8-10 minutes till it thickens slightly. Keep aside.

5. To serve, cut koftas into two. Boil the gravy separately, and pour in a serving dish. Arrange the koftas on the gravy and microwave for a couple of minutes to heat the koftas. Serve immediately with rice or bread.

Mushroom and Pea Curry

Mushrooms and peas are simmered in a delicious thick curry, flavoured with whole spices.

Serves 4

200 gm button mushrooms - trimmed and cut into quarters (2 cups)

or 1 cup tinned mushrooms, ½ cup boiled or frozen peas

3 tbsp oil, 1 tbsp butter

½ tsp cumin seeds (*jeera),* 1 bay leaf (*tej patta*)

2 black cardamoms (*moti illaichi),* 2 cloves (*laung*)

2 onions - chopped finely (1 cup)

1½ tsp ground coriander (*dhania powder*)

½ tsp red chilli powder, ½ tsp garam masala

¼ tsp ground turmeric (*haldi*), ¼ tsp dry mango powder (*amchoor*)

1¼ tsp salt, or to taste, 2 pinches each of pepper and sugar

¼ cup tomato puree

2 tbsp cashews ground to a paste with 3 tbsp water

1½ cups milk

1. Boil 2-3 cups water with 1 tsp salt. Add chopped mushrooms. After the boil comes again, keep on heat for a minute. Remove from heat and drain the water. Add fresh water and strain again. Keep aside.

2. Heat butter. Add the mushrooms and saute for 2-3 minutes on medium heat till water evaporates. Add the peas. Add 2 pinches each of salt, pepper and sugar. Stir for 2 minutes and keep aside.

3. Heat oil in a heavy bottomed pan. Add cumin, bay leaf, cardamoms and cloves. When cumin turns golden, add onions and stir fry till light golden.

4. Reduce heat. Add ground coriander, red chilli powder, garam masala, turmeric, mango powder and salt. Stir fry till onions turn golden brown.

5. Add tomato puree. Cook on low heat for about 5 minutes till oil surfaces. Add cashew paste and stir to mix well. Add milk, stirring continuously. Stir till it boils.

6. Add mushrooms and peas. Boil. Cover and simmer on low heat for 8-10 minutes, till oil surfaces and the gravy turns thick. Serve hot with breads like *chappatis or nans.*

Hyderabadi Subz Korma

Serves 4

4 baby corns - cut into thick slices, 6 small florets of cauliflower

5-6 French beans - chopped, 1 carrot - diced into ½" pieces

75 gm *paneer* - cut into ½" pieces

1½ tbsp ghee, 4 cloves (*laung*), 1" piece cinnamon (*dalchini*)

2 green cardamoms (*chhoti illaichi*), ½ tsp cumin seeds (*jeera*)

3 onions - ground to a paste

2 tsp ginger-garlic-green chilli paste

1 tsp salt, ½ tsp garam masala, ¼ tsp chilli powder, ¼ tsp pepper

½ cup milk, ½ cup coconut milk, 2 tbsp cream

1. Heat ghee, add cloves, cinnamon, cardamoms and cumin seeds. When cumin seeds crackle, add the onion paste and cook till onions turn light golden. Add the ginger-garlic-green chilli paste and cook for a minute. Sprinkle a tbsp water and stir for ½ minute.

2. Add carrot, beans, cauliflower and baby corns. Mix well. Stir for 2-3 minutes. Add salt, garam masala, chilli powder and pepper. Stir to mix well. Add ¼ cup water. Cover and cook on low heat till the vegetables are soft.

3. Add milk, coconut milk, cream and *paneer*. Cook on low heat for 1-2 minutes. Garnish with coriander leaves and serve hot.

Tandoori & Kadhai

Stir Fried Mixed Vegetables

Mixed vegetables cooked in cream and delicately flavoured with freshly ground black peppercorns.

Serves 4-6

150 gm (2 small) carrots, 150 gm green beans - cut into 1"/2.5 cm slanting pieces

½ cup boiled peas, 3 tbsp oil

3 onions - cut into fine rings (1 cup), 1 tbsp shredded ginger

½ tsp garam masala, 1¼ tsp salt, or to taste, 1 tsp ground coriander

½ tsp red chilli powder, ½ cup cream, 1 tsp lemon juice

PASTE

1 green chilli, optional, 1"/2.5 cm piece ginger

1 tbsp chopped fresh coriander, 1 tsp cumin seeds (*jeera*), 3-4 peppercorns

GARNISH

some grated cheese or *paneer*

1. Peel and chop carrots into slanting pieces. Microwave covered beans and carrots together with a sprinkling of water for 4 minutes, or till soft. Alternatively, steam or boil them till soft.

2. Grind all ingredients of the paste together. Heat oil. Add onions. Cook till brown. Add the ground paste. Cook for 1 minute. Add shredded ginger. Add the carrots, beans and peas.

3. Add salt, ground coriander, garam masala and red chilli powder. Mix well. Add 1/3 cup cream. Cover and cook for 2-3 minutes. Sprinkle lemon juice. Transfer the hot vegetables to a serving dish. Garnish with some grated cheese or *paneer* and serve hot with *chappatis*.

Kadhai Paneer

Fenugreek seeds and garlic are used to flavour this quick, yet exotic dish of paneer. Experiment this recipe with fried potato fingers as a substitute of paneer to get kadhai aloo.

Serves 6

250 gm *paneer* - cut into long thin fingers

2 green capsicums - cut into thin long pieces (1 cup)

2 dry, red chillies, 4 tbsp oil

1½ tsp coriander seeds *(saboot dhania)*

¼ tsp fenugreek seeds *(methi dana),* 1 tbsp dry fenugreek leaves *(kasoori methi)*

½ tbsp crushed garlic, 1 tbsp ginger-chopped, 3 tomatoes - chopped (1½ cups)

¾ tsp salt, or to taste

GARNISHING

1"/2.5 cm piece ginger - finely shredded

1. Coarsely grind dry, red chillies and coriander seeds together. Keep aside. Heat oil. Reduce heat. Add fenugreek seeds. Wait for a few seconds till they turn brown.

2. Add crushed garlic and cook till light brown. Add ground red chillies and coriander seeds. Stir. Add chopped ginger. Cook for 30 seconds.

3. Add chopped tomatoes and dry fenugreek leaves. Stir fry for about 5-7 minutes till oil separates. Add salt and green capsicums. Stir for a minute.

4. Add *paneer*. Cook for 2-3 minutes. Transfer to a serving dish. Garnish with shredded ginger. Serve hot with *paranthas*.

Tandoori Vegetables with Barbecue Sauce

Assorted vegetables smeared with a ginger-garlic flavoured yogurt paste and barbecued in a grill or a tandoor, which is a clay oven. These are wonderful when served with a sauce.

Serves 4

2 boiled potatoes (200 gm), 2 green peppers, 250 gm *paneer*, 1 onion

8 cherry tomatoes or 1 large tomato, 200 gm (10-12) button mushrooms

MARINADE

1 cup thick yogurt - hung for 10 minutes, 2 tbsp thick cream

½ tsp black salt, ½ tsp garam masala, ½ tsp red chilli powder, ¾ tsp salt, or to taste

BARBECUE SAUCE

4 tbsp oil, 8-10 flakes garlic - crushed (1 tbsp)

2 onions - very finely chopped, 1 cup tomato puree

½ tsp chilli paste or paprika, 2 tsp worcestershire sauce, 2 tsp soya sauce

½ tsp pepper, ½ tsp salt, or to taste, ½ tsp sugar, 1 cup water

1. Cut *paneer* and green peppers into large (1½"/4 cm) cubes. Leave cherry tomatoes whole but if the tomato is large, cut it into 8 pieces and remove the pulp. Trim the ends of the stalks of mushrooms, leaving them whole. Boil the potatoes, cut into cubes and fry till golden. Cut onion into four and separate.

2. Mix all ingredients of the marinade in a large bowl. Add *paneer* and vegetables. Marinate for 30 minutes. Arrange them on greased skewers. Place skewers on a greased wire rack.

3. Grill skewers in an oven at for about 8-10 minutes or roast in a gas tandoor. If you do not posses skewers, place the marinated vegetables directly on the grill brushed with some oil.

4. For the barbecue sauce, heat oil in a wok or a deep pan. Add garlic. Stir. Add onions and cook till brown. Add tomato puree and chilli paste. Mash onions and cook for 5 minutes till well blended.

5. Add soya sauce, worcestershire sauce, salt and pepper. Add water. Boil. Simmer for 5 minutes.

6. To serve, spread the hot sauce in a platter. Keeping the vegetable skewers on the sauce, pull out the skewers carefully to get an arranged line of vegetables on the sauce. Serve hot with rice.

Kadhai Mushrooms

A semi dry preparation of fresh mushrooms flavoured with ground coriander and fenugreek seeds.

Serves 4

200 gm fresh button mushrooms

1 green pepper - cut into 1 inch/2.5 cm pieces

2 onions - finely chopped (1 cup)

1"/2.5 cm piece ginger, 5-6 flakes garlic

3 tomatoes - chopped finely (1½ cups), 1-2 dry, whole red chillies, optional

1 tbsp coriander seeds *(saboot dhania)*, ¼ tsp fenugreek seeds *(methi dana)*

1 tbsp dry fenugreek leaves (*kasoori methi*)

1 tsp salt, or to taste

1 small tomato - cut into two halves, to garnish

2 green chillies - cut into thin long strips, optional

4 tbsp oil

1. Dry roast 1 tbsp dry fenugreek leaves on a *tawa*/griddle for 2 minutes on low heat till dry. Crush to a powder. Keep aside.

2. Grind ginger and garlic to a paste. Grind together, dry, whole red chillies and coriander seeds coarsely. Wash mushrooms well in plenty of water to remove any dirt. If mushrooms are small, keep them whole, if big, cut into halves. Wipe dry.

3. Heat 4 tbsp oil. Add mushrooms. Cook on medium heat, stirring occasionally, for 10 minutes till they turn brown and get cooked. Remove mushrooms from oil.

4. In the same oil, add fenugreek seeds. When they turn golden, add chopped onions and stir till light brown.

5. Add ginger-garlic paste. Cook for ½ minute. Add coriander-chilli powder. Add chopped tomatoes. Cook for 7-8 minutes, till oil separates. Add salt.

6. Add green peppers. Stir well. Add ¼ cup water. Add the cooked mushrooms and dry fenugreek leaves powder. Stir-fry for 2-3 minutes. Remove from heat. Garnish with tomato halves and slit green chillies. Serve with any type of bread.

Tandoori Arbi

Colocasia (arbi), makes an excellent side dish. Carom seeds aid the digestion of this vegetable, besides lending it's flavour to it.

Serves 6

500 gm colocasia *(arbi)* - 2"/5 cm long

1 cup yogurt - hung for 30 minutes

1 tbsp *tandoori or chaat masala*

1 tsp carom seeds *(ajwain)*

4 tbsp oil

2 onions - sliced (1 cup)

1 tsp ground coriander *(dhania powder)*

½ tsp garam masala

½ tsp dried mango powder *(amchoor)*

¼ tsp salt, or to taste

½ tbsp shredded ginger

1. Boil colocasia in salted water for 10-12 minutes till done. Remove from heat. Strain. Peel colocasia. Cut each into two pieces. Flatten each piece slightly.

2. Hang yogurt in a muslin cloth for about 30 minutes to let the liquid drain out. Mix 1 tbsp oil and *tandoori masala or chaat masala* to yogurt. Add ½ tsp crushed carom seeds also. Marinate the colocasia pieces in it for 15-20 minutes.

3. Brush the oven rack with some oil. Arrange the colocasia on the rack. Keep in a moderately hot oven at 190°C/375°F for 20 minutes, till the yogurt dries up and forms a coating. Remove from the oven and keep aside.

4. Heat 3 tbsp oil in a non stick pan. Reduce heat. Add ½ tsp carom seeds. After a few seconds when they turn golden, add sliced onions. Cook till onions turn light brown. Add the ground coriander, garam masala, dry mango powder and salt. Add the colocasia pieces.

5. Add the shredded ginger. Mix well. Stir fry for 3-4 minutes, adding a few teaspoons of oil, if it sticks to the pan. Remove from heat. Serve hot with onion rings and lemon wedges as a side dish.

Green Beans with Sesame Seeds

Sesame seeds spark the look and flavour of this ordinary vegetable. Remember to cut the beans into slightly longer pieces, about 2 inch/5 cm, to make them look more appetizing.

Serves 4

200 gm French beans - threaded and cut into 2"/5 cm long pieces

1 tomato - quartered (cut into 4 pieces)

2 tbsp dried fenugreek leaves (*kasoori methi*)

2 tbsp oil

1 tsp sesame seeds - dry roasted, to garnish

SPICE MIXTURE
(GRIND TOGETHER WITH A FEW TBSP OF WATER)

2 tsp sesame seeds (*til*)

1 tsp cumin seeds (*jeera*)

1 tsp ground coriander (*dhania*)

½ tsp red chilli powder

¼ tsp turmeric (*haldi*), 1 tsp salt, or to taste

1 big onion - chopped roughly (¾ cup)

2 flakes garlic

1. To prepare the spice mixture, grind onion with cumin seeds, sesame seeds, coriander powder, red chilli powder, garlic and turmeric with a little water to a fine paste in a coffee or spice grinder.

2. Heat 2 tbsp oil in a pan or a wok. Reduce heat. Add the spice mixture and fry for about 2 minutes, stirring continuously.

3. Add tomato pieces, beans and fenugreek. Stir fry for 5 minutes.

4. Cover and cook for 10-15 minutes or till the beans turn soft. Do not overcook them. Serve sprinkled with a few roasted sesame seeds with any type of bread.

Besani Matar

A dry preparation of peas coated with gram flour and tossed with onion rings.

Serves 4

3 tbsp oil

2 cups shelled peas - boiled or frozen

1 tsp cumin seeds (*jeera*)

3 onions - cut into rings, ½" piece ginger - finely chopped

2 tbsp gram flour (*besan*), ¾ tsp garam masala, ½ tsp red chilli powder

1½ tsp coriander (*dhania*) powder, ¾ tsp salt or to taste

2 tbsp fresh coriander - chopped

2 tomatoes - puree in a mixer

1 green chilli - deseeded & slit lengthwise, optional

1 tsp sesame seeds (*til*) - roasted on a tawa for 2 minutes till golden

1. Heat 3 tbsp oil in a *kadhai*, add cumin seeds. Let it turn golden. Add onion rings and stir till golden. Add ginger & saute over medium heat for ½ minute.

2. Add chick pea flour and saute on low heat for 2-3 minutes till gram flour turns fragrant.

3. Add pureed tomatoes, garam masala, red chilli powder and coriander powder. Saute for 3-4 minutes till puree turns dry. Add green chillies and coriander.

4. Add the boiled green peas and mix well. Add salt. Saute for 6-8 minutes. Transfer to a serving dish and sprinkle sesame seeds. Serve.

Tandoori Cauliflower

Whole cauliflower is baked with a ginger-garlic flavoured yogurt masala stuffed within the florets. Onion rings and fresh coriander topping adds to the taste.

Serves 8

3 small cauliflowers, each about 350 gm

MARINADE

1½ cups thick yogurt - hung for 30 minutes to give about ¾ cup hung yogurt

2 tbsp ginger-garlic paste

2 tsp *tandoori masala*

¼ tsp salt, or to taste, 2 pinches of turmeric for colour, ½ tsp paprika or degi mirch

2 tbsp oil

TOPPING

2 tbsp oil

4-5 small onions - cut into fine rings (1 cup), ¼ cup tomato puree

3-4 tbsp chopped fresh coriander, 1 green chilli - deseeded and chopped

salt to taste, 1 tsp *tandoori masala*

1. Boil 5-6 cups of water in a large pan with 2 tsp salt. Add the cauliflowers to the boiling water. Cook till it turns barely tender. Do not cook for too long. Remove from water and dry well on a clean kitchen napkin. Keep aside.

2. Mix all ingredients of the marinade in a bowl. Apply the marinade on the cauliflower, inserting some marinade inside the florets. Turn the cauliflower and insert some marinade from the backside also. Marinate the cauliflowers for at least 1 hour.

3. Place the marinated cauliflowers on a grill rack and cook in a hot oven at 200°/400°F till crisp and golden. Remove and keep on the serving platter.

4. To prepare the topping, heat 2 tbsp oil in pan. Add onion rings. When they start turning brown, add tomato puree. Stir. Add fresh coriander, green chillies and *tandoori masala*. Adjust salt and seasonings.

5. To serve, spread some onion topping on the grilled cauliflowers. Heat in a microwave or an oven. Serve hot with rice or bread.

Broccoli Spears

Broccoli florets with long stalks are flavoured with carom seeds and barbecued.

Serves 4

500 gm (2 medium heads) broccoli - cut into medium sized florets with long stalks

2 tsp salt, 1 tsp sugar

1ST MARINADE

juice of 1 lemon (3-4 tsp)

¾ tsp carom seeds *(ajwain)*

1 tsp salt and ½ tsp red chilli powder

2ND MARINADE

1 cup thick yogurt - hung for 15 minutes or more

½ cup thick cream

2 tsp ginger paste

½ tsp red chilli paste, optional

¾ tsp salt, 1 tsp *tandoori masala*

1. Boil 5-6 cups of water in a large pan. Add 2 tsp salt and 1 tsp sugar to the water. Add broccoli pieces to the boiling water. Boil. Keep on boiling for 2 minutes. Drain. Wipe the pieces well with a clean kitchen towel till well dried.

2. Spread the broccoli on a flat plate and sprinkle the ingredients of the 1st marinade. Marinate the broccoli for 15 minutes.

3. Drain the broccoli of any excess liquid. Mix all the ingredients of the 2nd marinade. Add the broccoli to it and mix well. Check the salt and add more if needed. Keep in the refrigerator till the time of serving.

4. Brush the grill of the oven or gas tandoor with some oil. Place the broccoli spears on it and barbecue them in a gas oven for 10 minutes or bake in a preheated electric oven at 210°C/410°F only for 10 minutes. Do not over cook it turns too dry. Serve hot as a side dish.

Balti Aloo

*A perfect combination of five seeds are popped into hot oil to impart all their flavour.
Fresh coriander leaves enhance the taste and look of this humble potato dish.*

Serves 4

4 medium (375 gm) potatoes, 2 medium onions - sliced (¾ cup)

3 tbsp oil

½ tsp cumin seeds *(jeera)*, ½ tsp fennel seeds *(saunf)*, ¼ tsp nigella seeds *(kalonji)*

¼ tsp mustard seeds *(rai)*, 2 pinches of fenugreek seeds *(methi dana)*

4-6 flakes garlic - crushed (1 tsp) 1"/2.5 cm piece ginger - cut into match sticks

½ tsp turmeric *(haldi)*, 1-2 dry, red chillies, a few curry leaves or fresh coriander leaves

salt to taste, 1 tsp *chaat masala*

1. Peel, wash and cut potatoes into ¼"/6 mm thick, round slices.

2. Heat oil in a non stick wok or a skillet. Reduce heat, collect all seeds —
    cumin, fennel, onion, mustard and fenugreek seeds, and add all together to
    the oil. Cook for ½ minute till the fennel seeds start changing colour.

3. Add garlic and ginger, stir fry for 1 minute. Add onions, stir fry until onions
    turn light golden. Add turmeric and dry red chillies. Stir. Add fresh coriander
    or curry leaves. Stir.

4. Add potatoes and salt. Mix well. Keeping the heat very low, cover tightly with
    a lid, and cook for 10-12 minutes or until the potatoes are tender. Uncover
    and add *chaat masala*. Adjust the seasonings. Transfer to a serving platter
    and serve hot as a side dish.

Achaari Bhindi

Serves 4

500 gm lady fingers (*bhindi*), 1 tsp ginger paste, ½ tsp red chilli powder
1 tsp coriander (*dhania*) powder, ½ tsp amchoor, ½ tsp garam masala
¾ tsp salt, or to taste, 2 tomatoes - chopped finely
1 tsp lemon juice

ACHAARI SPICES
a pinch of asafoetida (*hing*), 1 tsp fennel (*saunf*)
½ tsp mustard seeds (*rai*), ½ tsp onion seeds (*kalonji*), 2 tbsp oil

1. Wash bhindi and wipe dry. Cut the tip of the head of each bhindi, leaving the pointed end as it is. Now cut the bhindi lengthwise from the middle making 2 thin pieces from each.

2. Heat oil in a *kadhai*. Add bhindi. Cook for 8-10 minutes. Spread bhindi in a single layer while cooking it. Keep aside.

3. In a small bowl put 2 tbsp oil and all the achaari spices. Cook for 2 minutes. Remove from fire.

4. To the bhindi, add achaari spices and all the remaining ingredients. Mix very well. Cook for 2 minutes. Serve.

Legumes & Pulses

Dal Tempered with Peppers & Mushrooms

Mushrooms are sautéed along with some ginger-garlic paste and added to cooked pulses. The diced green peppers add the desired crunch and colour to the yellow dal.

Serves 4

1 cup yellow split peas *(channe ki dal)*

½ tsp turmeric powder *(haldi)*, 1½ tsp salt, or to taste

2 tsp ghee or butter, 3-4 cloves *(laung)*, 1 bay leaf *(tej patta)*

TEMPERING

3 tbsp oil

1 onion - chopped finely (½ cup), 1 tomato - chopped finely (½ cup)

60 gm mushrooms - chopped (½ cup), 1 green pepper - chopped finely

1 tsp ginger-garlic paste, ½ tsp red chilli powder, ½ tsp garam masala

1 tsp ground coriander *(dhania powder)*

1. Pick, clean and wash the pulses in 2-3 changes of water. Add turmeric, salt, cloves, bay leaf, ghee or butter and 4 cups of water. Give it a boil. Keep on low heat for about 15 minutes. Remove from heat.

2. Heat oil in a deep pan. Add onions. Cook till they turn brown. Add tomatoes. Cook for 2-3 minutes on low heat. Add ground coriander and garam masala. Cook for 30 seconds.

3. Add mushrooms. Cook for 3-4 minutes on medium heat till they get cooked. Add ginger-garlic paste and green peppers. Stir for a few seconds. Remove from heat. Add the cooked yellow split peas. Mix well. Serve hot with steamed rice.

Dal Makhani

Serves 4-5

1 cup whole black beans (*urad sabut*)

2 tbsp red kidney beans (*rajma*)

1 tbsp *channe ki dal,* 2 tbsp desi ghee

1½ tsp salt, 5 cups of water, 1 cup ready-made tomato puree

¼ tsp jaiphal powder, ½ tsp garam masala

1½ tbsp dry fenugreek leaves (*kasoori methi*)

2-3 tbsp butter, preferably white

GRIND TO A PASTE

2 dry, whole red chillies, preferably Kashmiri red chillies - deseeded & soaked for 10 minutes and then drained, 1" piece ginger, 6-8 flakes garlic

ADD LATER

½ cup milk mixed with ½ cup cream or well beaten malai

1. Wash the dals and red kidney beans, and soak in water overnight.

2. Drain water. Wash several times in fresh water, rubbing well, till the water get clear.

3. Pressure cook dal with 5 cups water, 2 tbsp ghee, salt and ginger-garlic-chilli paste. After the first whistle, keep on low flame for 30 minutes. Remove from fire. After the pressure drops, mash the hot dal a little. Keep aside.

4. To the dal in the cooker, add tomato puree, dry fenugreek leaves, garam masala and jaiphal powder.

5. Add butter. Simmer on medium flame for 20 minutes, stirring dal occasionally. Remove from fire. Keep aside to cool till the time of serving.

6. At the time of serving, add milk mixed with cream to the dal. Keep dal on fire and bring to a boil on low heat, stirring constantly. Mix very well with a *karchi*. Simmer for 2 minutes more, to get the right colour and smoothness. Remove from fire. Serve.

Note: Originally the dal was cooked by leaving it overnight on the burning coal angeethis. The longer the dal simmered, the better it tasted.

Sambhar

Sambar is a hot & sour dal of Southern India. It features three main ingredients —
toor/arhar dal (pigeon peas), tamarind pulp, and a special spice powder called sambhar
powder. The tamarind pulp may be increased if you like it more sour.

Serves 4

1 cup chopped mixed vegetables - beans, potato, lady's finger, brinjal, capsicum, carrots

2 green chillies - slit lengthways, 1 onion - cut into slices (½ cup)

½ cup pigeon peas (*arhar dal*)

3 tsp *sambhar powder*, ½ tsp turmeric *(haldi)* powder

lemon-sized ball of tamarind *(imli)*, or 1 tbsp tamarind pulp

salt to taste

2-3 tbsp chopped coriander leaves to garnish

TEMPERING

2 tbsp oil

½ tsp mustard seeds *(sarson),* 2 pinches asafoetida *(hing)* powder

¼ tsp fenugreek seeds *(methi dana),* ½ tsp cumin seeds *(jeera)*

1 dry red chilli, a few curry leaves

1. Wash and boil pigeon peas with 2½ cups water. Reduce heat, cover and simmer till well blended. If using tamarind pods, soak tamarind in 1 cup of hot water and extract pulp.

2. Cut beans into 1"/2.5 cm long pieces, potato, brinjal and capsicum into 1"/2.5 cm cubes, carrot into round thick slices, leaving lady's fingers whole.

3. Heat oil. Add all the ingredients of the tempering together. When the mustard seeds splutter, add the sliced onions and cook till golden. Add slit green chillies and the chopped vegetables. Fry for 3-4 minutes.

4. Add the tamarind pulp, salt, turmeric and *sambhar powder*. Cover and simmer on low heat till the vegetables are tender.

5. Add the cooked pigeon peas. Boil and then simmer for 5 to 10 minutes on low heat till everything blends. Garnish with chopped coriander leaves. Serve hot with plain boiled rice or lemon rice.

Masala Channe

Chick peas, commonly known as kabuli channe in India, are relished with fried bread called 'Bhaturas'. There are many different ways of cooking channas, but this one is flavoured with black cardamoms and cumin.

Serves 6

200 gm (1 cup) dried chick peas *(kabuli channe)*

1 tea bag, 6 tbsp oil

½ tsp cumin seeds *(jeera),* 2-3 black cardamoms *(moti illaichi)*

1 large onion - chopped (¾ cup), 2 tomatoes - chopped (1 cup)

½ tsp garam masala, 1 tbsp shredded ginger

1 tbsp ground coriander *(dhania powder),* 1 tsp dry mango powder *(amchoor)*

¾ tsp red chilli powder, salt to taste, ½ tsp garam masala

GARNISH

green chillies, onion rings, tomato & lemon wedges

1. Cover dried chick peas well with water in a bowl, stand overnight. Drain and rinse with fresh water. Drain again. Add 3-4 cups water and the tea bag. Boil. Simmer till done. Remove tea bag.

2. Strain the boiled chick peas, reserving the water.

3. Heat 3 tbsp oil. Add chick peas without the water to the hot oil and stir fry for 5 minutes. Remove from pan and keep the fried chick peas aside.

4. Heat 3 tbsp more oil in a clean pan. Add cardamom pods and cumin. When cumin turns golden brown, add onions and stir fry till onions turn light brown. Add ground coriander, dry mango powder and red chilli powder. Stir till onions turn deep brown, but take care not to burn them.

5. Add tomatoes, garam masala and shredded ginger. Cook till tomatoes get well blended and oil surfaces. Add the fried chick peas and stir fry for 2-3 minutes. Gradually add the liquid of the boiled chick peas, adding a little at a time. When all the liquid is over, simmer on low heat for 15-20 minutes.

6. Serve garnished with slit green chillies, onion rings, tomato and lemon wedges.

Red Lentils with Spinach

Red lentils are cooked along with spinach which enhances the taste and nutritive value of the lentils.

Serves 4

1½ cups (125 gm) chopped spinach, 1 cup red lentils *(dhuli masoor ki dal)*

1 flake garlic - finely chopped, optional, 1"/2.5 cm piece ginger - grated

½ tsp turmeric *(haldi)*, 1½ tsp salt, or to taste

TEMPERING

3 tbsp oil or ghee, 1 onion - chopped (½ cup), 1 tomato - chopped (½ cup)

½ tsp cumin seeds *(jeera)*, ½ tsp garam masala, ½ tsp red chilli powder

½ tsp ground coriander *(dhania powder)*, 1/8 tsp dried mango powder *(amchoor)*

1. Pick, clean and wash dal in 2-3 changes of water. Wash chopped spinach in plenty of water. Mix lentils, spinach, garlic, ginger, turmeric powder and salt in a deep pan. Add 3 cups of water to the lentils. Give one boil and then keep on low heat for 12-14 minutes, till the lentils turn soft but not mushy. Remove from heat. Keep aside.

2. To temper the dal, heat oil or ghee in a small pan. Reduce heat and add the cumin seeds. Let the seeds turn golden. Add the onions and stir till onions are well browned. Add the tomatoes and cook for 2-3 minutes. Add garam masala, ground coriander and dried mango powder.

3. Remove from heat and add the red chilli powder. Pour the hot oil over the lentils. Mix gently. Serve hot with *nans* or any other flat bread.

Raitas, Salads Chutneys & Pickles

Tempered Cabbage & Coconut Salad

South Indians love coconut in all their dishes. The brown skin of the coconut kernel should be removed before grating the coconut for this salad. A combination of red and green cabbage may be used to make the salad more interesting.

Serves 4

125 gm plain yogurt (½ cup)

1½ cups shredded green cabbage

½ cup freshly grated coconut, 1 tsp finely grated ginger

2 green chillies - deseeded & chopped, optional

salt to taste

TEMPERING

1 tbsp oil, ½ tsp mustard seeds (*sarson*)

½ tsp cumin seeds (*jeera*), a pinch of red chilli powder

1. Whisk yogurt. Keep it in a large mixing bowl. Toss cabbage, coconut, ginger, green chillies and salt in the yogurt. Keep aside.

2. Heat 1 tbsp oil, reduce heat. Add cumin seeds and mustard seeds. When they crackle, remove from heat. Add a pinch of red chilli powder and pour over the prepared yogurt. Serve.

Raita Anaarkali

A sweet and sour raita with fresh kernels of pomegranate (anaar). Slices of boiled potatoes are arranged around the yogurt. The tamarind chutney is very simple to prepare and it can be stored for many days in the freezer. You may have this raita even without the tamarind chutney.

Serves 4

500 gm plain yogurt (2 cups)

1 cup fresh pomegranate kernels - (*annar daane*)

½ tsp red chilli powder, ½ tsp salt or to taste, 1 tsp ground, roasted cumin (*bhuna jeera*)

2 small potatoes - boiled and cut into slices, a few fresh coriander leaves - to garnish

1 tbsp tamarind (*imli*) chutney

TAMARIND (*IMLI*) CHUTNEY

1 tbsp tamarind pulp, 3 tbsp sugar, or to taste, ½ cup water

½ tsp ground ginger (optional)

¼ tsp black salt, salt or to taste, ½ tsp ground, roasted cumin (*bhuna jeera*)

1. Mix all ingredients of the tamarind chutney. Keep on heat and stir well to mix. Cook till a saucy consistency is reached. Cool. The chutney will thicken as it cools.

2. Beat the yogurt well till absolutely smooth. Add the pomegranate kernels, salt, cumin seeds and red chilli powder to the beaten yogurt. Transfer to a serving dish. Surround the dish with boiled potato circles.

3. Pour a little chutney on the potato slices. Arrange a small bunch of whole coriander leaves in the centre. Garnish with kernels of pomegranate.

Hari Chutney

A green (hari) chutney prepared from fresh coriander and mint leaves. As long as this chutney is there with my meals, I can enjoy anything without creating a fuss. My favourite!

Serves 4

½ cup mint leaves *(pudina leaves)*

1 cup fresh coriander *(hara dhania)* - chopped along with stems

2 green chillies, 1 onion - chopped (½ cup)

1½ tsp dried mango powder *(amchoor),* 1½ tsp sugar

½ tsp salt, or to taste

1. Wash coriander and mint leaves. Grind all the ingredients together to a smooth paste. Serve with snacks or with meals.

Aam ka Achaar

Makes 1 kg

1 kg raw mangoes

250 gm mustard oil

½ tsp hing, 1 large pod or 50 gm garlic - chopped finely

150 gm salt, 50 gm red chilli powder, 25 gm turmeric powder *(haldi)*

25 gm fenugreek seeds *(methi daana)* - dry roast on a tawa & grind to a powder

1. Cut the mangoes into small pieces. Remove the seed.
2. Heat ½ of the oil, add hing and garlic.
3. Add salt, red chilli powder, haldi and roasted methi daana powder.
4. Cool the masala and add mangoes.
5. Mix it and fill in a jar. Keep in the sun for 2 days.
6. Heat the rest of the oil to smoking point. Cool it and add to the pickle in the jar.
7. Keep the pickle in the sun, shaking the jar daily once.

Cucumber and Dill Raita

A lovely combination of greens - cucumber and dill in yogurt, makes a perfect accompaniment to any meal. The freshly ground coarse peppercorns enhance the taste.

Serves 4

500 gm plain yogurt (2 cups)

¾ cup thickly grated, unpeeled cucumber

1 tsp powdered sugar

½ tbsp dried dill flakes

½ tsp peppercorns - coarsely ground

salt to taste

1. Beat yogurt well till smooth. Grate thick shreds of a small unpeeled cucumber on the grater.

2. Add all the ingredients to the yogurt. Mix well and transfer to a serving bowl. Sprinkle some dill flakes on top. Keep in the fridge till serving time.

Coconut & Peanut Chutney

This authentic chutney, originating from Southern India, is superb with all types of bean and lentil appetizers. Fresh coconut is traditional, but to make the procedure simpler, you may opt for the desiccated coconut instead.

Serves 6

½ cup freshly grated or desiccated coconut

½ cup roasted peanuts (without the red skin)

1 green chilli - chopped, 1 onion - chopped (½ cup)

½ tsp salt, or to taste, ½"/1 cm piece ginger

1 cup yogurt - approx.

TEMPERING

1 tbsp oil, 1 tsp mustard seeds *(sarson)*

1-2 dry, red chillies - broken into bits, a few curry leaves

1. Grind all ingredients of the chutney adding enough curd to get a thick paste of soft dropping consistency. Keep aside in a bowl.

2. To temper the chutney, heat 1 tbsp oil. Add mustard seeds. When they splutter, add broken red chillies and curry leaves. Remove from heat and pour the tempered oil on the chutney. Mix lightly.

Garlic Pickle

A very easy pickle to prepare. It helps in also digesting the food besides adding zest to the food.

Makes 500 gm

½ kg garlic - peeled
½ cup mustard oil
½ cup vinegar
25 gm (5 tsp) salt
2 tsp ground turmeric *(haldi)*
4 tsp red chilli powder
4 tsp ground mustard *(rai powder)*

1. Peel the garlic. Heat mustard oil to smoking point. Reduce heat. Add all the garlic together. Cook for 2 minutes on low heat. Let it cool.

2. Heat vinegar in a separate pan. Remove from heat. Add salt, turmeric, red chilli powder and ground mustard.

3. Mix the garlic in oil to the *masalas* in vinegar. Fill it in dry bottles. This pickle can be eaten immediately also.

Sweet Mushroom Pickle

A very interesting sweet and sour pickle with fresh mushrooms.

Makes 500 gm

500 gm button mushrooms

50 gm (1 pod) garlic - ground to a paste, 2 inch/5 cm piece ginger - ground to a paste

¾ cup oil

a pinch of asafoetida *(hing)*, 4 tsp red chilli powder

5 tsp mustard *(rai)* powder, 5 tsp salt, ½ cup raisins *(kishmish)*

GRIND TOGETHER
2 tsp fenugreek seeds *(methi dana),* 2 tsp sesame seeds *(til)*

BOIL TOGETHER
1 cup vinegar, 3-4 tbsp ground jaggery *(gur)*

1. Boil 4-5 cups water with 2 tsp salt. Add mushrooms and boil for about 5 minutes till a little soft. Drain and dry on muslin cloth for 5-6 hours.

2. Heat oil in a deep pan. Fry the garlic paste till light golden, then add ginger and fry till golden brown. Add asafoetida. Add the ground sesame and fenugreek seeds. Remove from heat. Add red chilli powder, ground mustard and salt. Mix the mushrooms with this masala.

3. In a pan heat vinegar. Add jaggery and cook on low heat till jaggery dissolves. Remove from heat and add kishmish.

4. Add to the mushrooms. Mix well. Put in a jar. Consume within 2 weeks or refrigerate if it has to be kept for a longer period.

Rice & Breads

Bhatura

These are deep fried breads, which puff up on frying. The semolina makes it crisp, so these breads are crisp on the outside and soft from inside. These are mostly served with masala chick peas.

Serves 4

250 gm (2 cups) plain flour *(maida)*

100 gm (¾ cup) semolina *(suji)*

½ tsp baking soda

½ tsp salt

1 tsp sugar

½ cup yogurt (approx.)

oil for deep frying

1. Soak semolina for 15 minutes in about ¼ cup water, which is just enough to cover it.

2. Sift salt, baking soda and flour. Add sugar, semolina and yogurt to the sifted flour. Knead with some warm water to make a smooth dough of rolling consistency. Brush the dough with oil. Keep covered in a warm place for 3-4 hours.

3. At serving time, make 8-10 balls. Roll each ball to an oval shape. Pull from one side to get a pointed tip.

4. Heat oil. Deep fry bhaturas in medium hot oil. Remove from oil before they turn brown.

5. Serve with masala channas give on page 64.

Panfried Cauliflower Paranthas

These are pan fried flat breads which are stuffed with a spicy cauliflower filling. In India we relish them with just plain yogurt and some pickle or a chutney, during the winter months. My son, Anurag, likes to add a dollop of butter on the paranthas and that's a treat for him!

Serves 4

DOUGH

2 cups whole wheat flour *(atta)*, ½ tsp salt, about ¾ cups water to knead

FILLING

2 cups grated cauliflower

1 tsp salt, ½ tsp garam masala, ½ tsp paprika or red chilli powder

1"/2.5 cm piece ginger - grated finely, 2-3 tbsp chopped, fresh coriander

oil or butter for frying

1. Mix salt and whole wheat flour in a shallow pan or a food processor. Add enough water to get a dough of rolling consistency. Knead well till smooth. Cover and keep aside for at least 30 minutes.

2. To prepare the filling, add all ingredients to the grated cauliflower and mix well. Keep aside for 15 minutes. Squeeze the cauliflower well after 15 minutes to drain out the excess water.

3. Make 2 marble sized balls of the dough. Roll out each ball into very thin rounds. Spread some filling on one rolled out dough and cover with the other round. Press the edges well to join.

4. Carefully pick up the *parantha* and put it on a hot griddle or a shallow pan. When the underside is cooked, turn to cook the other side. Smear some oil or butter on the *parantha*. Trickle some oil on the sides too, around the edges. Turn the *parantha* to make it brown. Similarly make other *paranthas*. Serve with plain yogurt and some pickle or chutney.

Spinach–Carrot Rice

A healthy combination of spinach and rice! It's not only delicious, but the green spinach ribbons scattered on white rice makes it very tempting. The carrot shreds enhance the look further.

Serves 4

1 cup basmati rice - soaked for about 1 hour

350 gm spinach *(paalak)* - discard stems & cut leaves into thin strips (2 cups)

2 carrots - grated (1 cup)

4 tbsp oil

½ tsp fennel seeds *(saunf),* 2 brown cardamoms *(moti illaichi)*

1 stick cinnamon *(dalchini),* 2 cloves *(laung)*

1 onion - sliced finely (½ cup)

1½ tsp salt, or to taste, ¼ tsp red chilli powder or paprika

2 tsp lemon juice

1. Soak rice for about 1 hour.

2. Heat oil in a large, heavy bottomed pan. Add fennel seeds, cardamoms, cinnamon and cloves. Wait till fennel seeds just change colour.

3. Add onions and stir fry till transparent. Add spinach and grated carrots. Stir fry for 1 minute.

4. Drain the water from the rice and add to the spinach. Add salt and red chilli powder. Add 2 cups water and lemon juice. Stir gently to mix well.

5. Boil. Reduce heat and cook covered, for 12-15 minutes or until the rice is done. Fluff it up with a fork to separate the grains. Serve hot with a refreshing *raita* (yogurt).

Qabooli

A vegetable biryani with split gram lentils. The word qabooli means acceptable or palatable and the rice is definitely delicious.

Serves 8

3 cups long grain rice - soak for 20 minutes

½ cup yellow split gram lentils (*channe ki dal*) - soak for 20 minutes

1 cup yogurt

3 onions - finely sliced, 1 tsp ginger paste, 1 tsp garlic paste

¼ tsp turmeric powder, 1 tsp red chilli powder

juice of 2-3 lemons, a few sprigs of fresh green coriander - chopped

a few fresh green mint leaves - chopped, 4 green chillies - coarsely chopped

¾ cup oil, 2 tbsp ghee, ¼ cup milk

GRIND OR CRUSH TO A POWDER

½" piece cinnamon (*dalchini*), 2-3 green cardamoms (*illaichi*)

½ tsp black cumin seeds (*shah jeera*), ½ tsp peppercorn (*sabut kali mirch*)

1. Boil 1 cup water with ¼ tsp salt and a pinch of turmeric. Add the dal and cook on low heat till tender.

2. Boil a large panful of water (10-12 cups). Add 2 tsp salt to the boiling water. Add rice and stir to mix well. Boil till 80% cooked (soft, yet chewy). Strain. Leave in the strainer for a minute and then spread the parboiled on a tray.

3. Heat oil in a *kadhai*. Fry the onions till golden brown. Remove half of the onions for later use and set aside. Add ginger and garlic to the onions in the kadhai and stir. Add turmeric and stir.

4. Add yogurt and stir briskly and cook for about 5 minutes. Add the lentils and red chilli powder. Cook for two-three minutes. Check salt and add to taste.

5. Take a heavy-bottomed pan and brush the bottom with a little oil. Spread half of the parboiled rice. Spread the lentils over the rice. Sprinkle the ground spices. Also spread half of the mint, coriander and green chillies and lemon juice. Cover with remaining rice. Sprinkle the milk, the fried onions & balance of the mint, coriander and the lemon juice and dot the rice with ghee.

6. Cover with foil. Keep on a hot tawa for 5 minutes on medium heat. Reduce heat. Let the rice cook on low heat for 10 minutes till the rice is cooked and steaming hot.

Makai Khichdi

Simple and wholesome with plenty of flavour and eye-appeal – enjoy the sweetness of corn in this delicious khichdi.

Serves 2

1¼ cups rice, 3 tbsp ghee or butter

a pinch of asafoetida (*hing*), 2" piece of ginger - chopped

2-3 green chillies - remove seeds & chop finely

3 tsp salt, 2 tbsp chopped coriander leaves, 1 tsp lemon juice

1 tsp turmeric powder (*haldi*), 1 tsp cumin seeds (*jeera*)

1 cup corn kernels (*bhutte ke daane*), 3½ cups water for cooking rice

1. Wash and soak the rice for half an hour.

2. Heat ghee in a saucepan. Add cumin seeds. Cook till it starts to change colour.

3. Add hing and then add chopped ginger, chopped green chillies and turmeric. Mix well and cook for 2-3 minutes.

4. Add cooked corn and 3½ cups water and bring to a boil. Add rice, salt, coriander and lemon juice, mix and cook covered on slow flame till rice is cooked and the khichdi is of the right consistency.

5. Garnish with garam masala and red chilli powder. Serve hot with yogurt, papad and pickle of your choice.

Tip: Consistency of khichdi is a matter of personal preference. If you want khichdi to be runny, add a little more water.

Spinach Parantha

Chopped spinach and flour, flavoured with some carom seeds are kneaded together to a dough. A pinch of turmeric added to the dough makes the parantha more pleasing to the eyes.

Serves 4

2½ cups whole wheat flour (*atta*)

1½ cups finely chopped spinach

1 tsp salt

½ tsp turmeric (*haldi*), ½ tsp red chilli powder

½ tsp garam masala, ¾ tsp carom seeds (*ajwain*)

ghee or oil for frying

1. Wash spinach leaves and place them in a shallow pan or a food processor. Add all other ingredients except the flour and ghee for frying.

2. Add the flour on top. Mix well. Add just enough water to make a firm dough of rolling consistency. Knead well till smooth and elastic. Cover and keep aside for at least 30 minutes for the dough to become soft and elastic.

3. Take small portions of the dough, roll them out into round chappatis and smear with ghee. Fold into half. Again fold into half to form a triangle. Roll out once more to a big triangular *parantha*.

4. Put one *parantha* at a time on a heated tawa (griddle), cook one side and turn over. Add a little ghee from the sides and some on the top surface. Turn and cook till it gets a nice brown colour. Cook on medium heat. When ready it should be crisp. Similarly, make more *paranthas*.

Afghani Nan

Nans are oblong oven baked flat breads. Traditionally they are baked in a clay oven called 'tandoor' but I have prepared them in an electric boiler with equal success.

Serves 4

2 cups (250 gm) plain flour (*maida*)

½ cup hot milk

½ tsp baking powder

½ cup warm water (approx.)

½ tsp salt

1 tsp nigella seeds (*kalaunji*) or 1 tsp black or white sesame seeds (*til*)

1. Heat milk and put it in a large, shallow pan or a mixing bowl. Add baking powder to the hot milk. Mix well and keep it undisturbed for 1 minute. Bubbles will start appearing on the surface.

2. Sift plain flour and salt together. Add flour to the hot milk in the pan or bowl. Mix well. Knead to a soft dough with enough warm water. Keep in a warm place for 3-4 hours to swell.

3. At serving time, make 6-8 balls of the dough. Roll out each ball to an oblong shape. Sprinkle some onion seeds or sesame seeds. Press the seeds with a rolling pin. Pull one side of the nan to give it a pointed end like the shape of the nan.

4. Apply some water on the back side of the nan. Press on the walls of a hot tandoor. Alternatively, cover the rack of the oven with an aluminium foil. Bake the nans in a very hot oven or broiler by keeping them on the foil. When light brown specs appear on the surface, turn the side of all the nans. Cook till done. Smear some butter on the hot nan and serve hot with *dals* or curries.

Subz Biryani

The term biryani is used to define a fragrant rice preparation which was very popular in the Moghul era. This vegetable rice is cooked with a fragrant biryani paste made from many flavourful seeds. Remember to cook biryani in a large, heavy bottomed pan.

Serves 6-8

2 cups basmati rice - soaked in water for 1 hour

100 gm carrots - cut into small cubes, 300 gm cauliflower - cut into small florets

10 french beans - cut into small pieces, 1 bay leaf (*tej patta*)

1/3 cup oil, 2 onions - sliced finely (1 cup)

3 tsp salt, or to taste, 1 tsp lemon juice

BIRYANI PASTE

6-7 flakes garlic, 1 inch/2.5 cm piece ginger

1 tsp fennel seeds (*saunf*), 1 tsp cumin seeds (*jeera*), 1 tsp ground coriander (*dhania*)

1 stick of cinnamon (*dalchini*), 3 cloves (*laung*), seeds of 2 green cardamoms (*illaichi*)

1. Grind all the 8 ingredients of the biryani paste together with a little water. Keep paste aside. Heat oil in a large, heavy bottomed pan. Add sliced onions, cook till golden brown. Remove from oil.

2. Add the ground biryani paste to the oil. Stir fry on low heat for 1-2 minutes. Add the vegetables and stir fry for 2-3 minutes.

3. Measure 4 cups of water (double the volume of rice) and add to the vegetables. Add salt and lemon juice. When water boils, drain the rice and add to the boiling water. Give it a boil. Reduce heat.

4. Cover the pan of rice with a small towel napkin and then with a well fitting lid. Keep some heavy weight on the lid. To reduce heat further, you may put a heavy griddle under the pan of rice. Cook for about 12-15 minutes, or until the rice is done. Fluff the rice with a fork, so that the grains separate. Serve after 10 minutes with plain yogurt.

South Indian Lemon Rice

Yellow rice flavoured with mustard seeds and lemon juice. Ground turmeric is used to give colour to it. Yellow split peas add crunch to the rice.

Serves 4

1 cup basmati rice

3 tbsp lemon juice, ¼ tsp ground turmeric (*haldi*)

½ tsp sugar, 1½ tsp salt, or to taste

TEMPERING

3 tbsp oil

1 tsp mustard seeds (*sarson*), 1 tbsp yellow split peas (*channe ki dal*)

3 dry, red chillies - broken into pieces, few curry leaves

1. Clean and wash rice. Boil 5-6 cups water in a large pan. Add rice. Boil till done. Strain the rice. Keep aside. Cool for ½ hour by spreading on a tray. Separate the rice grains with a fork.

2. Mix lemon juice, turmeric, salt and sugar together. Keep aside.

3. Heat oil in a large wok. Reduce heat. Add mustard seeds, dal and red chillies. Cook on very low heat till dal peas turn brown. Add curry leaves.

4. Add the lemon juice mixture. Add ¼ cup water. Cover and simmer on low heat till dal turns soft and the water dries. Run a fork through the boiled rice to separate the rice grains and add the rice to the lemon juice mixture in the wok. Stir gently to mix well. Serve hot with yogurt.

Desserts

Sandesh

Makes 4-5 pieces

1 litre full cream milk (5 cups), 2 tbsp vinegar, 2 tbsp water

7 tbsp powdered sugar or to taste, 2 tbsp cornflour

2 tbsp pistachio - grind to a powder, a few drops of green colour

GARNISH

a few whole pistachio pieces

1. Boil the milk. Mix vinegar in water and gradually add it to the milk till the milk curdles. Strain the *paneer/chhena* in a muslin cloth. Dip the *chhena* tied in the cloth in ice cold water for 10 minutes to stop further cooking. Hang the *chhena* in the cloth for 30 minutes to drain all water.

2. Grind *chhena*, sugar and cornflour in mixer till it is smooth. Transfer to a heavy bottomed *kadhai*.

3. Cook the *chhena* mixture for 8-10 minutes on low heat. The *paneer* should not change colour. It should turn dry and become thick.

4. Remove to a bowl, add powdered pistachio and green colour. Make round and flattened pieces. Decorate with pistachio. Refrigerate till serving time.

Nariyal ki Burfi

Serves 10

250 gm desiccated coconut (*nariyal ka bura*)

175 gm sugar (1 cup), ¼ cup water

250 gm *khoya* type (*pindi*) - mash roughly

2-3 drops or pinches of raspberry red colour

1. Heat a *kadhai* and warm *khoya* in it on low heat for 1 minute. Do not let the *khoya* change colour. Remove from fire and let it cool.

2. Heat water and sugar in saucepan. Cook for about 10 minutes till it forms one thread consistency (*ek taar ki chhanshi*). Remove from fire and let it come to room temperature.

3. Add desiccated coconut to the syrup. Mix well. Add *khoya* and mix well.

4. Divide the mixture into 3 parts. Spread 2 parts in a small greased tray or a tiffin box. Add colour to the last part and mix it well. Set it as the second layer on the white layer of burfi. Level it with the help of spoon and then keep aside for 1 hour to set. Cut into small square pieces.

Saffron Kulfi Falooda

The delicious Indian Ice cream topped with sweetened thin vermicelli.
Saffron lends it's flavour and colour to this most popular Indian dessert. Pistachios and
almonds add to the richness.

Serves 6-8

1 kg (4 cups) low fat milk

5 tbsp skimmed milk powder, 3 tbsp cornflour

¼ cup sugar, 6-7 strands saffron (*kesar*)

3-4 green cardamoms (*chhoti illaichi*) - crushed, 1 tbsp shredded pistachios (*pista*)

1 tbsp shredded almonds (*badam*)

FALOODA

1 cup thin rice vermicelli, 3-4 strands saffron (*kesar*)

3 tbsp sugar, 2 green cardamoms (*chhoti illaichi*)

1. Dissolve cornflour and milk powder in ½ cup milk to a paste. Heat the rest of the milk with sugar and saffron. Add the paste gradually, stirring continuously. Mix well. Add crushed seeds of green cardamoms. Boil. Simmer on low heat, for about 15 minutes till slightly thick.

2. Cool. Add pistachios and almonds. Fill in clean kulfi moulds and leave to set in the freezer for 6-8 hours or overnight.

3. To prepare the falooda boil 4 cups water. Add the rice vermicelli. Boil. Simmer on low heat for 2-3 minutes till the vermicelli turns soft and no crunch remains. Strain. Add cold water to refresh. Strain again.

4. Make a sugar syrup by boiling ¾ cup water, 3 tbsp sugar, saffron and green cardamoms together. Simmer for a couple of minutes. Remove from heat and put in the boiled vermicelli. Keep soaked in sugar syrup, in the refrigerator, till serving time.

5. To serve, remove the kulfi from the mould, cut into two halves lengthways and top with some falooda (without the syrup). Serve.

Gajar ka Halwa

Almost every home in India has a box stocked with this carrot pudding in winters. It is served hot during the cold winter months, when fresh, red carrots are in plenty.

Serves 4

500 gm carrots - grated into long shreds

1 cup milk

¼ cup sugar

2-3 tbsp ghee or unsalted butter

5-6 almonds (*badam*) - shredded

10-12 raisins (*kishmish*)

seeds of 3 green cardamoms (*illaichi*) - crushed

100 gm khoya - grated

1. Boil milk with crushed cardamom seeds in a clean wok or a deep pan. Add grated carrots and cook uncovered, stirring occasionally, till milk dries.

2. Add almonds and raisins. Stir for 1 minute. Add sugar. Cook till the mixture turns dry again.

3. Add ghee and stir fry for 10 minutes on low heat till ghee separates.

4. Add khoya and mix well for 2-3 minutes. Serve hot garnished with some nuts.

Kesari Phirni

A milk pudding cooked with ground rice paste and flavoured with saffron and green cardamoms.

Serves 6

3½ cups (700 gm) milk, 1/3 cup basmati rice

1/3 cup sugar (slightly less than ½ cup) or to taste

25 almonds - blanched and ground to a paste with some water

4 almonds (*badam*) - shredded

5-6 green pistachios (*pista*) - soaked, peeled and sliced

2 small silver leaves - optional

seeds of 2-3 green cardamoms (*chhoti illaichi*) - powder

1 drop kewra essence or 1 tsp ruh kewra

a pinch of yellow colour

DECORATION

a few rose petals - dipped in cold water, a few strands kesar - soaked in warm water

a few fresh anaar ke daane

1. Soak rice of good quality for about 2-3 hours and then grind very fine with 4 to 5 tablespoonfuls of cold water to a paste. (You may soak rice overnight & keep in the fridge.)

2. Dissolve the rice paste in ½ cup milk and make it thin.

3. Mix the rice paste with the remaining 3 cups milk in a heavy bottomed pan. Keep on fire and cook on medium heat, stirring continuously, till the mixture is of creamy consistency, about 5 minutes.

4. Add the kesar water or a drop of colour, sugar and cardamom powder and stir. Simmer till sugar is fully dissolved and then boil for 5-6 minutes on medium heat.

5. Remove from fire. Add almond paste. Mix well.

6. Add ruh kewra or the essence and half of the shredded almonds and pistachios.

7. Pour the mixture into 6 small earthern containers. Chill. Decorate each dish with a silver leaf, rose petals, kesar and the remaining shredded nuts. Top with some fresh anaar ke daane.

Zarda Pullao

Sweet rice flavoured with saffron and enriched with nuts is made on special occasions and festivals in India. It is important to soak the rice at least an hour in advance.

Serves 8

2 cups basmati rice - soaked for 1 hour

2 cups sugar

1 inch/2.5 cm piece of fresh or dried coconut - cut into small pieces, optional

4 green cardamoms (*chhoti illaichi*) - crushed

4 cloves (*laung*)

1 stick cinnamon (*dalchini*)

2 tbsp raisins (*kishmish*)

1 tbsp pistachio (*pista*), 2 tbsp almonds (*badam*)

4 tbsp desi ghee or oil

few strands saffron dissolved in 1 tbsp hot water

1. Boil 1½ cups of water with 2 cups of sugar and green cardamoms. Keep sugar syrup aside.

2. Heat ghee in a large, heavy bottomed pan. Add cloves, cinnamon, coconut, almonds and raisins. Fry for 30 seconds.

3. Drain the rice and add to the pan. Add 2½ cups of water. Boil. Add saffron along with the water. Cover with a tight fitting lid and cook the rice on very low heat till water dries up and the rice is almost done.

4. After the water dries up, add the prepared sugar syrup into the rice. Mix gently. Cook covered on very low heat till rice is completely done and all the water gets absorbed. Remove from heat. Keep covered in the pan for a few minutes. Fluff with a fork to separate the rice grains. Transfer to a rice platter and decorate with a silver leaf, a few pistachios and almonds.

Suji ka Halwa

Serves 4

1 cup semolina (*suji*)

6 tbsp of desi ghee or vanaspati ghee

1 cup sugar

1 cup milk

2 cups water

seeds of 4 green cardamoms (*chhoti illaichi*) - crushed

few strands of kesar

8-10 raisins (*kismish*)

8-10 almonds - cut into thin long pieces

1. Mix milk, water, crushed cardamoms, kesar and sugar.

2. Boil. Stir to dissolve the sugar. Keep aside.

3. Roast suji in a pan on medium flame till fragrant. Do not let it turn brownish. This will take about 6-7 minutes.

4. Heat ghee in a *kadahi*. Fry semolina on low heat it turns golden. Add kishmish.

5. Add milk mixture, stirring continuously for 7-8 minutes till the *halwa* leaves the sides of the *kadahi*.

6. Remove from fire.

7. Keep in a serving dish. Decorate with silver leaf, shredded almonds and pista. Serve hot.

INTERNATIONAL CONVERSION GUIDE

These are not exact equivalents; they've been rounded-off to make measuring easier.

WEIGHTS & MEASURES

METRIC	IMPERIAL
15 g	½ oz
30 g	1 oz
60 g	2 oz
90 g	3 oz
125 g	4 oz (¼ lb)
155 g	5 oz
185 g	6 oz
220 g	7 oz
250 g	8 oz (½ lb)
280 g	9 oz
315 g	10 oz
345 g	11 oz
375 g	12 oz (¾ lb)
410 g	13 oz
440 g	14 oz
470 g	15 oz
500 g	16 oz (1 lb)
750 g	24 oz (1½ lb)
1 kg	30 oz (2 lb)

LIQUID MEASURES

METRIC	IMPERIAL
30 ml	1 fluid oz
60 ml	2 fluid oz
100 ml	3 fluid oz
125 ml	4 fluid oz
150 ml	5 fluid oz (¼ pint/1 gill)
190 ml	6 fluid oz
250 ml	8 fluid oz
300 ml	10 fluid oz (½ pint)
500 ml	16 fluid oz
600 ml	20 fluid oz (1 pint)
1000 ml	1¾ pints

CUPS & SPOON MEASURES

METRIC	IMPERIAL
1 ml	¼ tsp
2 ml	½ tsp
5 ml	1 tsp
15 ml	1 tbsp
60 ml	¼ cup
125 ml	½ cup
250 ml	1 cup

HELPFUL MEASURES

METRIC	IMPERIAL
3 mm	1/8 in
6 mm	¼ in
1 cm	½ in
2 cm	¾ in
2.5 cm	1 in
5 cm	2 in
6 cm	2½ in
8 cm	3 in
10 cm	4 in
13 cm	5 in
15 cm	6 in
18 cm	7 in
20 cm	8 in
23 cm	9 in
25 cm	10 in
28 cm	11 in
30 cm	12 in (1ft)

HOW TO MEASURE

When using the graduated metric measuring cups, it is important to shake the dry ingredients loosely into the required cup. Do not tap the cup on the table, or pack the ingredients into the cup unless otherwise directed. Level top of cup with a knife. When using graduated metric measuring spoons, level top of spoon with a knife. When measuring liquids in the jug, place jug on a flat surface, check for accuracy at eye level.

OVEN TEMPERATURE

These oven temperatures are only a guide. Always check the manufacturer's manual.

	°C (Celsius)	°F (Fahrenheit)	Gas Mark
Very low	120	250	1
Low	150	300	2
Moderately low	160	325	3
Moderate	180	350	4
Moderately high	190	375	5
High	200	400	6
Very high	230	450	7

Herbs & Spices

	ENGLISH NAME		HINDI NAME
1	Asafoetida	1	Hing
2	Bay Leaves	2	Tej Patta
3	Cardamom	3	Elaichi, Chhoti Elaichi
4	Cardamom, Black	4	Moti Elaichi
5	Carom Seeds	5	Ajwain
6	Chillies, Green	6	Hari Mirch
7	Chillies, Dry Red	7	Sukhi Sabut Lal Mirch
8	Chilli Powder, Red	8	Lal Mirch Powder
9	Cinnamon	9	Dalchini
10	Cloves	10	Laung
11	Coriander Seeds	11	Sabut Dhania
12	Coriander Seeds, ground	12	Dhania Powder
13	Coriander Leaves	13	Hara Dhania
14	Cumin Seeds	14	Jeera
15	Cumin Seeds, black	15	Shah Jeera
16	Curry Leaves	16	Kari Patta
17	Fennel Seeds	17	Saunf
18	Fenugreek Seeds	18	Methi Dana
19	Fenugreek Leaves, Dried	19	Kasuri Methi
20	Garam Masala Powder	20	Garam Masala
21	Garlic	21	Lahsun
22	Ginger	22	Adrak
23	Mace	23	Javitri
24	Mango Powder, Dried	24	Amchur
25	Melon Seeds	25	Magaz
26	Mint Leaves	26	Pudina
27	Mustard Seeds	27	Rai, Sarson
28	Nigella, Onion Seeds	28	Kalaunji
29	Nutmeg	29	Jaiphal
30	Peppercorns	30	Sabut Kali Mirch
31	Pomegranate Seeds, Dried	31	Anardana
32	Sesame Seeds	32	Til
33	Saffron	33	Kesar
34	Turmeric Powder	34	Haldi

BEST SELLING COOKBOOKS BY

SNAB
Excellence in Books

Different ways with PASTA

Burgers & Sandwiches

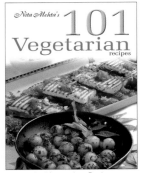
101 Vegetarian Recipes

Chocolate Cookbook

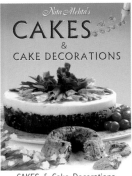
CAKES & Cake Decorations

Best of INDIAN COOKING

SPECIAL Non-Vegetarian Recipes

MEDITERRANEAN Cooking

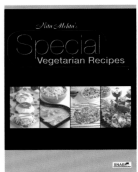
SPECIAL Vegetarian Recipes

Cooking for GROWING CHILDREN

Dadi Maa Ke Nuskhon Ka Khazana

EVERYDAY Cooking

MEXICAN cooking for the Indian kitchen

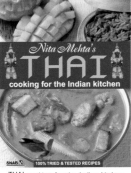
THAI cooking for the Indian kitchen

101 MICROWAVE Recipes

FOOD from around the WORL

BEST SELLING COOKBOOKS BY

Fish & Prawns

Delhi Ka Khaana

CONTINENTAL cooking for the Indian kitchen

MULTICUISINE Cookbook

Vegetarian CONTINENTAL

Vegetarian SNACKS

Soups & Salads

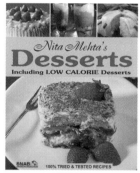

DESSERTS

The Best of NON-VEGETARIAN

Vegetarian MUGHLAI

Vegetarian CHINESE

ZERO OIL Cooking

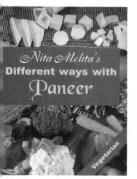

Different ways with PANEER

Great INDIAN Cooking

LOW CALORIE cooking for the Indian kitchen

101 CHICKEN Recipes

BEST SELLING COOKBOOKS BY

SNAB Excellence in Books

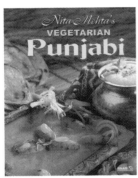
Vegetarian PUNJABI

CHINESE cooking for the Indian kitchen

ITALIAN cooking for the Indian kitchen

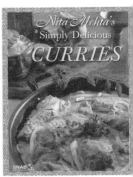
Simply Delicious CURRIES

The Best of CHICKEN & PANEER

SUBZIYAAN

TANDOORI cooking in the OVEN

Tempting SNACKS

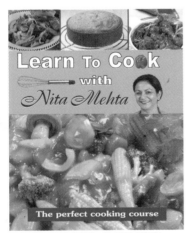
LEARN TO COOK with NITA MEHTA

Flavours of INDIAN Cooking

Oats Breakfast Cookbook

Learn to Cook CHOCOLATE

Learn Food Styling, Garnishing & Table Laying

Learn to Cook PIZZA & PASTA

Learn to Cook LEBANESE